HOT LINE

Grief

by Laurie Beckelman

Series Consultant
John Livingstone, M.D.

Crestwood House
Parsippany, New Jersey

In memory of my grandparents and uncle

Author's Note: Many teenagers generously shared their thoughts and experiences with me. The quotes in this book are based on their stories.

Published by Crestwood House, an imprint of Silver Burdett Press.
A Simon & Schuster Company
299 Jefferson Road, Parsippany, NJ 07054

First Edition

Design: Lynda Fishbourne, Hemenway Design Associates
Packaging: Prentice Associates Inc.

Photos:
SuperStock: Cover, PhotoEdit: (Cleo Photography)4,
(Tony Freeman)7, 10, 18, 34, 37, (Dennis MacDonald)7,
(Richard Hutchings)15, 40, (David Young-Wolff)32, 46,
(Michael Newman)27, 43, The Image Bank: 13, 22, 29, 44

Printed in the United States of America
10 9 8 7 6 5 4 3 2 1

Library of Congress Cataloging-in-Publication Data
Beckelman, Laurie.
        Grief / by Laurie Beckelman. — 1st ed.
            p. cm. — (Hot line)
        Includes bibliographical references and index.
        ISBN 0-89686-847-8   ISBN 0-382-24958-5 pbk.
        1. Grief — Juvenile literature. 2. Loss (Psychology) — Juvenile literature.
3. Bereavement — Psychological aspects — Juvenile literature.
4. Death — Psychological aspects — Juvenile literature. [1. Grief. 2. Death.]
I. Title. II. Series: Beckelman, Laurie.
Hotline
BF575.G7B423   1995
155.9'37 — dc.20   94-45692

Summary: A discussion of the process and stages of grieving and the losses that may cause grief. Offers advice that can help teens understand and tolerate these normal but difficult feelings.

HOT LINE

Grief

CONTENTS

Everyone else seemed so normal while I was falling apart inside. I felt so alone I wanted to scream. But instead I went downstairs and tried not to cry.

Torn Hearts

"After my dad moved out, I didn't want to do anything," recalls David. "I went to school — you know, went through the motions — but nothing felt real. When I got home, all I wanted was to be left alone."

"We went to my uncle's house after my grandmother's funeral," says Karen. "People kept coming by to pay their respects. First they'd say how sorry they were, but then they'd act like nothing had happened. They'd all talk about normal things — and my mother and uncle joined in. I couldn't stand it. Everyone else seemed so normal while I was falling apart inside. I felt so alone I wanted to scream. But instead I went downstairs and tried not to cry."

"After Jeff broke up with me, I was a real mess," says Marsha. "For weeks I'd cry at the littlest thing. I felt terrible about myself, about the way I looked, and about my life. Everyone kept telling me to just get over it, but I couldn't. I felt like someone had taken a big chunk out of my heart and thrown it away."

David, Karen, and Marsha have each experienced a **major loss.** Something of value to them is now gone from their lives. Day in and day out, many teens have similar experiences. Their parents separate or divorce. They lose cherished friends or relatives to death. They discover that they or someone they love is seriously ill. Their relationships break up, disaster claims prized possessions, or they fail to reach goals that meant the world to them.

As different as these types of loss are, they can all cause **grief**. Grief is a state of mind and body. It is the normal but painful emotional response to loss, and it touches every life. At some point, each of us loses someone or something we deeply love. Most of us also face moments of failure that shake our very sense of who we are. "Swimming was my whole life," says Roy. "From the time I was a little kid I took lessons. My dream was to make the Olympics. But it turns out that I wasn't even the best in my state. When I started losing state and national competitions, I felt like my life was over. I didn't know anything could hurt so much." Roy had lost his most precious possession: his sense of who he was and could be. As a result, he felt grief.

Grief is one of our most painful emotions, but it is

Grief forces us to take time out from our everyday life so that we can address the question "What now?"

also one of the most healing. It is our body's way of closing an emotional wound. As we grieve, we learn to tolerate our losses and to build new lives for ourselves. Roy needed time to accept that he would not be an Olympic swimmer and to address the question "What now?" His grief, as painful as it was, helped him do this. It forced him to take time out from his everyday life so that he could absorb this change in self-image and set a new direction. Similarly, David, Karen, and Marsha needed time to mourn their losses and to adjust to lives without a live-in dad, a grandmother, or a boyfriend.

Just as a wound of the flesh takes time to heal, so does one of the heart. The deeper the wound, the longer the healing process. Grief over a major loss does not pass in minutes or hours or even days. Rather, we measure the journey through grief in months or years. Grief does not feel the same at the beginning of the journey as it does at the end. Grieving is a process that goes through predictable stages. It takes us from the first shock of loss through **despair** to finding new meaning in life despite our sadness. There is no shortcut through this process, but knowing what it is and that it is normal can help you understand your grief — and yourself — better.

We can rarely prevent the losses that cause us grief. Nor can we stop the feelings that follow. But we can learn to tolerate those feelings and to reach out for the support that can lessen the pain. In so doing, we become stronger. We grow because of grief.

The Meaning of Loss

When David's parents divorced, sadness and anger took over his mind. Concentrating became impossible. For weeks after the divorce, he found himself staring off into space when he should have been working. He'd lash out in anger at the smallest insult.

Joni's parents also divorced, but she had a very different reaction. She found that relief quickly replaced sadness. "When my dad first moved out, I was really upset," says Joni. "But then I realized that the knot in my stomach that I'd had every night for as long as I could remember was gone. My parents used to fight all the time, and I hated it. Once my dad left, the house was peaceful. I'm not so nervous and scared any more. But I miss him, and I still feel sad about what my family could have been."

David's and Joni's experiences illustrate an important point: People can react very differently to similar losses. Their parents' divorces meant different things to David and Joni. The significance that David and Joni placed on their losses and the changes the losses caused in their lives — not the events themselves — shaped their reactions.

The personal meaning we attach to a loss determines the strength and duration of our grief. What might seem a minor loss to one person can feel major to another. Similarly, one person's major loss might cause little more than a ripple of unhappiness for someone else.

For example, Karen's friend Grace thought that Karen's response to her grandmother's death was "overdoing it just a little." When Grace's grandmother died, Grace hadn't been nearly as upset. But Karen was very close to her grandmother, while Grace had a distant relationship with hers. Karen and her grandmother had baked together, had gone out to lunch, and had even talked about boys. Grace knew her grandmother mainly from postcards that would arrive from all over the world. Her grandmother liked to travel and was rarely around to spend time with Grace.

People often mistakenly use their own experiences to judge what's right for someone else. If they have not had a similar experience, they might make assumptions about how someone should feel. If you are grieving a loss, you may find that some of your friends or relatives ex-

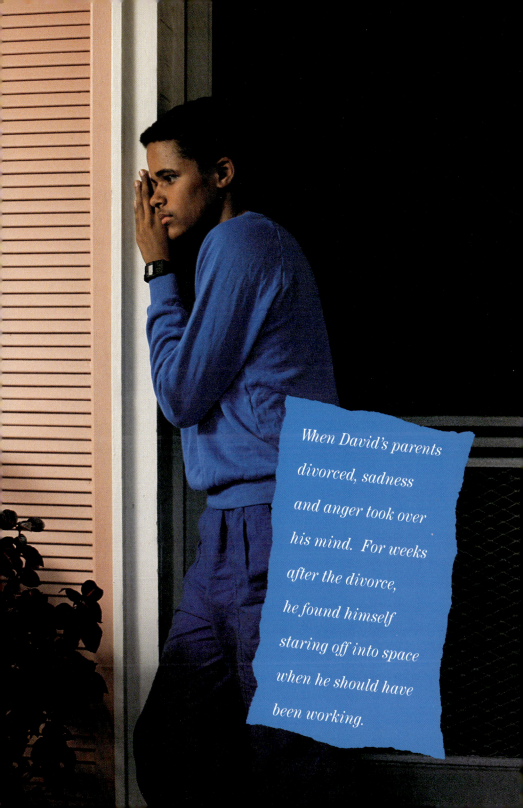

When David's parents divorced, sadness and anger took over his mind. For weeks after the divorce, he found himself staring off into space when he should have been working.

pect you to react differently than you do. You may get the message that you should be "over it already." Or maybe you are hearing just the opposite. Peter's father died when he was nine. Two days after the funeral, Peter was out playing softball with some friends. "My aunt really laid into me when I came in," remembers Peter. "She said I wasn't showing enough respect for my father's memory. She didn't understand that hitting that ball was my way of dealing with the pain. I was so mad about my father being gone that I had to take it out on something. Besides, playing ball made me feel like I was still close to my dad. It was something we always did together."

There is no one "right" way to feel or express grief. As you read this book, remember that

■ The reaction you have to a loss is unique to you.

■ Other people's experiences can help you understand your own, but they are not identical. Even members of the same family may react differently to the death of someone they love because they all shared different relationships with that loved one.

■ Grief does not follow a timetable. Grief over a major loss can last as little as several months or as long as several years. There is no "right" length of time to grieve. However, grief rarely passes in only a few days or a week.

■ You are the biggest expert on how you feel. The goals of this book are to help you tune into your feelings, to reassure you that they are normal, and to share ideas that have helped other people cope with grief in the hope that the ideas will help you, too.

Grief over a major loss can last as little as several months or as long as several years. There is no "right" length of time to grieve.

The Journey Through Grief

"**M**y mother's best friend picked me up at school and told me that a fire had destroyed my house," says Annette. "At first, it was like getting kicked in the stomach. Then I thought, 'This can't be happening,' and I began to panic."

Like all emotions, grief affects our bodies, feelings, and thoughts. Annette's sensation of having the wind kicked out of her, her thoughts that the fire couldn't have really happened, and her feelings of panic and fear are all parts of her reaction to her loss. They are typical of **early grief**, the first part of the **grieving process**.

The grieving process is like an emotional bridge between our past and our future. We want to hold onto the past — our world as it was before the loss — yet we need to let go. The grieving process helps us make the transition from holding on to letting go. Through grief, we come to tolerate our loss. We enter the future with greater self-knowledge and inner strength.

Dr. Elizabeth Kübler-Ross, an expert on death and dying, was the first person to describe the grieving process. In her work with dying patients and their families, she recognized that people go through predictable stages in response to death. These are

■ *Shock and denial.* When they first hear the news, people refuse to believe that someone they love has died or is dying or that they themselves have a fatal illness.

■ *Anger.* People rage against the unfairness of the situation, blaming everyone from doctors to God to themselves for what has happened.

■ *Bargaining.* Often, people try to strike a bargain with the universe to make things right again. For example, a

Some grief experts believe that the mini-grief reactions we experience from day to day are rehearsals for the larger losses that will someday come.

girl whose younger brother has cancer may pray for his recovery, promising that she'll never tease him again in return. Such bargaining takes place after someone has died, too. Only over time do we let go of the hope that our wish to have someone back will come true.

■ *Despair.* As the reality of a loss sinks in, so does the bottomless sorrow of despair. We yearn for what we have lost and take little pleasure in what we still have. The lost person or possession truly seems or is irreplacable.

■ *Acceptance.* Over time, despair lifts. We find that we have the strength to carry on despite our loss. We may even find that we are stronger and more **resilient** because of it.

The stages of grief are not like chapters of a book that neatly follow one another. They overlap. For example, feelings such as disbelief and anger, which are most common early in grief, can pop up later, too. This is normal.

Since Dr. Kübler-Ross did her pioneering work, many other specialists have studied the grieving process. Grief experts now recognize that people experience the reactions Dr. Kübler-Ross described in response to any major loss, not just death. Indeed, some believe that we go through a mini-grief reaction whenever we experience a loss, no matter how small.

Think of what happens when you fail a test you thought you'd done well on, for example. Your first response may be shock at your poor grade, followed by denial: "The teacher must have made a mistake." When you realize that your grade is not a mistake, anger sets in. You may be mad at your teacher for making the test too hard, mad at your father for making you help clean the garage when you needed to study, or mad at yourself for not doing well. Despair sets in as you acknowledge your failure and begin to worry that you'll flunk the course.

Depending on how important the test was to you, these feelings may last for just a second, a few hours, or even a few days. But chances are they will pass quickly. You'll accept your grade and move on. If you're lucky, you will have learned something from your loss and that lesson will help you do better the next time around.

Some grief experts believe that the mini-grief reactions we experience from day to day are rehearsals for the larger losses that will someday come. If we learn to handle these minor losses, they say, we will be better prepared to respond to the major ones.

Knowing that we have successfully survived past losses helps us believe in our capacity to cope. This faith in ourselves is an important support when we are grieving a major loss. Minor losses also expose us to the type of emotional pain grief brings. This makes the pain less frightening. However, minor losses do little to prepare us for the *intensity* of our feelings when major loss strikes.

The death or illness of a sibling or friend can make you feel very vulnerable. You may worry that something as bad could happen to you.

"It Can't Be!"

"**M**y dad was the one who told me that I needed a kidney transplant," says Julie. "I laughed. I told him that was a *really* sick joke, even though I knew how ill I was and that the doctors had said I might need a transplant. My dad told me he wasn't joking and tried to hug me, but I pushed him away. My heart was beating like wild and I felt like I was going to explode. I called my father a liar. I yelled it over and over: Liar! Liar! Liar!"

Shock, denial, anger, sorrow, numbness, fear — all these feelings can rush into the void that loss creates. In the days following a major loss, you may feel as if you are on an emotional roller coaster. You may be as numb as a zombie one minute, then overcome with sorrow the next. You may be furious at a parent or sibling, only to have your fury give way to a desperate need to hold that person close and to agree with him or her about everything.

Fear or panicky feelings are common after

a major loss. Your world is suddenly less safe and dependable than it was. It is normal to feel scared. These feelings may be especially strong if you have lost a parent or other caregiver. You may have very real concerns about who will take care of you. You may worry that your family will not have enough money to manage. Sharing these concerns with an adult you trust can help. He or she may have information that will reassure you.

The death or illness of a sibling or friend can also make you feel very vulnerable. You may worry that something as bad could happen to you. If, like Julie, you are dealing with your own illness, those worries about what will happen to you will be even stronger. Your body's response to loss may make them stronger yet.

Like any powerful emotion, grief triggers the **general adaptation response**, your body's one-size-fits-all response to any extra demand. Your heart may beat wildly; your muscles tense. You may sweat, feel short of breath, and breath rapidly. Your mouth may feel like cotton, your stomach as if you've been riding a roller coaster. You may have little interest in eating, or you may have trouble sleeping.

These reactions may start as soon as you hear of your loss or may hit once the reality of your situation sinks in. They will likely come in waves, lasting from minutes to hours and leaving you exhausted. Although these physical symptoms will become less frequent and less severe over time, the general adaptation response is triggered often during the grieving process. The loss is a threat to your well-being, and your body is alert, ready to respond to other dangers.

Just as these physical symptoms are protective, so are the shock and denial that are almost always the very first response to loss. They bolt the door of awareness, protecting us from a reality that may be too painful to know. Only slowly can we let in the truth of what has happened. Only slowly can we accept that we have lost something so central to our lives that we feel we have lost part of ourselves.

Even when the loss is expected, as when someone dies after a long illness, we often can't believe it has actually happened. "My brother had cancer," explains Marc. "When he died, I couldn't really believe it because I didn't feel anything. I mean, I *knew* he was dead, but my mind refused to accept it. It wasn't until the funeral that it really sank in."

Marc's experience is very common. Shock and denial, as well as the numbness that may alternate with strong feelings of anger, fear, and sorrow, generally fade within the first hours or weeks following a loss. They give way to an intense, sorrowful yearning for that which is gone.

Despair is the stabbing, seemingly bottomless sorrow that rules the first months of grieving. You may feel hopeless and depressed. Concentrating on schoolwork or hobbies may be impossible.

"All I Do Is Cry"

Kelly's friend Janet was hit and killed by a car as she was walking home from Kelly's house. Kelly explains how she's felt since the accident: "I cry a lot. I sit and do nothing a lot. I feel a sadness that just won't let go. It's like a choking collar that I'll have to wear forever."

The despair Kelly describes is common following a loss. Despair is the stabbing, seemingly bottomless sorrow that rules the first months of grieving. You may feel hopeless and depressed. Activities you usually enjoy may hold little interest or appeal. Concentrating on schoolwork or hobbies may be impossible. You may find that you are restless much of the time or **listless**; that you can't sleep or can't keep your eyes open; that the thought of food makes you sick or that you can't get enough to eat. You may find that life has lost all its color and detail, that you feel as if you will never survive this loss.

These symptoms of grief are very similar to those of **depression**. Someone who experiences symptoms of depression in response to loss is not ill, however. Just the opposite is true. Feeling this despair is a sign of health. It means that you are letting yourself grieve. Despair forces you to rethink what really matters to you. Painful though this is, it is the key to coming to terms with your changed life. By staying with rather than running from your feelings, you will discover your own emotional strength. You will learn that you can survive despite your loss.

There are two circumstances under which the symptoms of depression might signal a serious problem, however. If the symptoms go on without letup for more than six months, you may be stuck in this despair phase of the grieving process. You may need help to understand your feelings and thinking. Your pastor or rabbi or a licensed grief counselor or therapist may be able to help you.

You should also tell somebody if you feel suicidal. For some people, the feeling that they will not survive the loss gives way to the belief that they *should* not. They may have recurrent thoughts about suicide or death. They may think of death as a relief from pain or have recurring images of a specific plan to end their lives. If this happens to you, you should tell a parent, teacher, or other adult immediately. Grief does pass, even though it's hard to believe that it will. The pain you feel now will not rule the rest of your life.

Strong Feelings

The deepest despair usually lessens within the first three to six months of the grieving process. Of course, these feelings may pass more or less quickly depending upon how deeply you are grieving. Grief over a broken relationship may pass more quickly than grief over a death, for example.

As the depressionlike parts of despair lift, the sorrow continues. We may experience it as a heart-piercing yearning. We may cry, think nonstop about our loss, and go over and over the details of what happened and how it might have ended differently. We will feel many other strong emotions, too. These feelings, which are present in the earliest stages of grief, flare up time and again throughout the grieving process. They include

■ *Anger.* The anger that we feel in the very early stages of grief may continue to rear up as we move through the grieving process. We may feel angry at someone who has left us, even if that person has died. We may feel angry at ourselves for not having prevented the loss, even though we most likely could not have. We may feel angry at doctors, parents, God, or anyone else we hold responsible for allowing the loss to occur. What has happened to us is not fair. The rage we feel in response to such injustice is normal. We need to feel it and to share our feelings with others. But we also need to face the hurt, fear, guilt, and helplessness that often lie just below the surface of anger. As we confront these other emotions, our anger often lessens.

■ *Fear.* A major loss rips apart the fabric of our lives. It shakes our trust in the world. Fears for our own survival or for the safety and health of those close to us are normal at such times. We may not experience this fear consciously. Rather, we may find that we simply prefer to stay close to our parents, or that we become anxious if someone is late picking us up. We may become oversensitive to what others say, hearing rejection when none is intended. News of world disasters, such as floods or earthquakes, may distress us more than usual. As time passes, however, we realize that we will survive, as will those we love. We become less fearful.

■ *Guilt.* The author Christopher Leach, whose young son died, writes: "All who live with the memory of a dead loved one feel a measure of guilt. Not enough was said;

not enough was done." The feeling Leach describes may follow any major loss. Even when we know that we were not responsible for the loss, we may feel as if we were. We may think, "If only I'd been a better son (or sister, daughter, friend), this wouldn't have happened." Because brothers and sisters may sometimes wish one another ill, feelings of guilt can be especially strong when a sibling is sick or has died, even though we know it's not our fault. Teens with very ill siblings may also feel jealous of the attention their brothers or sisters get. This too can feed guilt.

■ *Loneliness.* If we have lost someone we love, we may miss him or her terribly. We may yearn to have him or her back. Sometimes we want so badly to regain what we have lost that we act on our hope of doing so.

Grief brings many confusing feelings. Sharing them with someone we trust often helps us feel better.

"I Kept Looking, but He Wasn't There"

"**A**fter my dad left, I'd go to this park where we used to play touch football on summer evenings," says David. "I kept thinking that maybe he'd just show up."

David's visits to the park were not crazy. They were a normal step in accepting the reality of loss. Not ready to let go of what has been lost, we seek to find it. We may do this again and again, in thought if not in action. Evidently we need to experience this rise and fall of hope many times before we can accept that we cannot recover what is gone.

The yearning to turn the clock back, to somehow find a happier ending, can give rise to the bargaining that Dr. Kübler-Ross identified as a common stage of grieving. For example, we may stop arguing with our siblings and start doing our chores in the hope of bringing our separated parents

David's visits to the park were not crazy. They were a normal step in accepting the reality of loss.

back together. Our bargaining may or may not be con-
scious. Sometimes we act on a hidden fantasy that what
we do can change what has happened. This "magical
thinking" is often connected to an unconscious belief
that we are responsible for our loss. As with searching
for what we have lost, we often repeat the bargaining
process many times before we can accept that we cannot
change what has happened.

Over time, we will stop trying to bargain with fate.
Our yearning will lessen. We will find that we have hours,
even days, when we do not think about our loss. As
Barbara Lazear Ascher, an author whose brother died of
AIDS, writes: "You learn that you can cry and stop and
laugh and . . . then cry again." Over time, the tears become less frequent, the laughter more so. We build a new
life, one that acknowledges our loss but is not ruled by it.
We are on our way to acceptance.

Acceptance

"One day about eight months after my grandmother died, I decided to bake the chocolate cake she always made," says Karen. "When I smelled the aroma of that cake baking, I felt as if I were back in my grandmother's kitchen. I could see Grandma sinking her cake tester into the cake and smiling with pride as she took it out of the oven. To my surprise, the feeling was happy as well as sad."

For Karen, the pain of grief had given way to the bittersweet tenderness of remembering. She was able to enjoy baking her grandmother's favorite cake and to take pleasure in her memories of the times Grandma had baked it for her. She even decided that she would bake the cake every year on her grandmother's birthday, as a tribute of her love. This decision made Karen feel good. She realized that she had ways of remembering her grandmother with more caring than pain.

Special occasions sometimes make Karen really miss her grandmother. But the pain of grief has mainly given way to the tenderness of remembering.

There are still times when the pain of her grandmother's death hits her once again, however. These usually come on special occasions she'd like to share with her grandmother, such as her birthday or the day she won a medal in gymnastics.

Chances are that Karen will feel these occasional pangs of grief throughout her life. Many people who have lost someone or something they deeply loved do. Sue is a grandmother whose brother died during World War II. "A childhood friend recently gave me some old photos she'd found. They were taken one summer when our two families were on vacation together," she says. "Seeing my young, handsome brother made me cry. After all these years, it can still hurt so much."

Although Karen and Sue both still sometimes feel pain over their losses, their pain does not interfere with their lives. They both have close, loving relationships with family and friends; they both take pleasure and pride in the activities that shape their days. When they remember the people they've lost, it's sad, things have changed, but that's OK. This is the sign of acceptance.

The pain we feel in response to loss is a measure of our capacity to care. It reflects our willingness to love or to work for something we believe in. We learn through grief that even when we lose the object of our love or fail to meet a goal, our capacity to love and to try remain.

This is the gift of the grieving process. It moves us beyond sorrow, fear, and anger. It reveals to us the inner strength that enabled us to love and to try and that will let us love and try again. Grief can actually expand our capacity to love. Once we have known our own pain, we are better able to understand someone else's. We are more capable of providing the support and **empathy** that build strong bonds between people.

Once we have known our own pain, we are better able to understand someone else's. We are more capable of providing the support and empathy that build strong bonds between people.

Softening the Pain of Grief

You cannot avoid or control the difficult feelings that come with grief. But you can help yourself tolerate them more easily. Here are some steps that grief counselors recommend.

■ *Let the feelings flow.* The feelings you experience when grieving are neither good nor bad. They just *are*. The best way to work them out is to let them flow.

■ *Cry.* If you feel like crying, do. Whether you are male or female, crying is a healthy, normal response to grief. Tears wash **toxins** out of the body, which might be why we feel better after a good cry.

■ *Share the feelings.* More than anything else, having people with whom you can share your feelings lightens the load of grief. Sharing your feelings can remind you that you are not alone, that you have people who love you and care. Sharing painful feelings can be hard.

You may be afraid that speaking of them will make them hurt more. Most people find that just the opposite is true, however. Talking helps them feel better even though nothing changes. This is most true when someone listens to them without trying to "fix" what's wrong. You can ask for this kind of listening. Telling the story of what happened, or sharing memories of someone you've lost, can also help you feel better. Each time we retell our story, it becomes a little more real to us, and we move closer to acceptance.

■ *Join a support group.* If you are mourning a death, if you are ill, or if your parents have divorced, you may be able to join a group of teens who are going through similar changes in their lives. Julie, the girl who needed the kidney transplant, found that talking to other teens like herself was the greatest help in coping with her illness. "They understood a lot of what I was feeling," she says. "They weren't afraid to hear about what was going on like some of my friends were. I could tell them anything."

■ *If you are religious, pray.* Many people find that their faith in God helps them make sense out of loss and is a comfort while they are grieving.

■ *Keep your routine as normal as possible.* This is likely to be a disorganized time in your life. Keeping your routine as normal as possible can help you structure your days and return a measure of certainty to your life.

People who are grieving often become forgetful and find that they cannot concentrate. This can hurt your schoolwork or other areas of your life. Try making lists of things you need to do or develop your own version of a piece of string around the finger to help you remember.

■ *Take care of your body.* The next chapter tells how.

Many people find that their faith in God helps them make sense out of loss and is a comfort while they are grieving.

Staying Healthy

When our bodies stay on alert for long periods of time, as happens during the grieving process, we can suffer health problems. The chemicals released in response to **stress** make the **immune system** function less effectively. This makes us more vulnerable to infectious diseases, such as the flu and colds. These and other minor problems, such as upset stomachs, headaches, and rashes, are common among people who have suffered a major loss. Some people who are grieving seem to have one health problem after another.

These health problems, even when minor, may be frightening. This is a time of great vulnerability and uncertainty in your life. You may have fears about your own health and safety, especially if you are mourning a death. It's always a good idea to see a doctor if you are worried about your health. A physical exam will let you know if you have any reason for concern.

There are also many things you can do to keep healthy during these very stressful times. Glen Davidson, chief of **thanatology** at Southern Illinois University School of Medicine, studied the health habits of grieving people. He found that the people who stayed physically healthy were most likely to do the following.

■ *Eat regular, well-balanced meals.* Your body needs a steady flow of energy to stay healthy. You can get this only from eating regularly. Your body also needs the nutrients that come with a balanced diet.

■ *Drink lots of fluids, but avoid alcohol or caffeine.* Every cell in your body needs water to function properly. Water is necessary to carry oxygen and nutrients to your cells, to remove waste products from your body, and for digestion, among other things. In times of stress, when you may be crying, urinating, and sweating more than usual (and therefore losing water), making sure that you drink enough fluids is important. However, alcohol and drinks such as cola, coffee, and tea that contain caffeine are **dehydrating** and should be avoided.

■ *Exercise.* Regular exercise has many benefits. It helps release tension and, by keeping you physically engaged, can provide a healing timeout from sorrow. **Aerobic exercise** has the further benefit of boosting levels of **endorphins**. These are brain chemicals that dull feelings of pain.

■ *Rest.* Grief is exhausting. Dr. Davidson found that grieving people who allowed themselves to rest or sleep when they felt tired stayed healthier than those who kept pushing themselves to stay active.

Taking care of your body in these ways will not make your grief go away. But it will help you cope more successfully with your strong feelings and increase the chances that you will stay healthy through the grieving process.

Grief is exhausting. Grieving people who allow themselves rest or sleep when they feel tired stay healthier.

When a Friend
Is Grieving

"**M**y friend Kirsten's mom died," says Allison. "She was sick for a long time and everyone expected it, but it was still really hard on Kirsten. I wanted to help her, but I didn't know how."

Many people, not just teens, don't know how to respond to a friend who is grieving. We're not used to seeing those we care about in such great pain. We want to help end their pain — and our own discomfort in seeing it. We may think, "If only I could come up with the right thing to say or do, everything would be OK again." But there is no "right thing" that will magically put an end to grief. As you know, grieving sets its own pace, and working through grief, not ending it, is the road back to wholeness.

This doesn't mean you can't help a friend who is grieving. Your friendship and your willingness to stand by your friend and to accept and tolerate his or her grief are great gifts that you can give. Just being there may not seem like much, but it is.

Too often, the discomfort of seeing someone else's pain is so great that people pull away. They may stop seeing the grieving person or show their uneasiness in less obvious ways. For example, after Karen's grandmother died, one friend kept telling her that if she just acted happy she'd start to feel happy. "My *friend* was the one who felt better when I acted like my old self," says Karen. "I didn't. I felt worse because I had to put on this act when all I really wanted was to say, 'I hurt *so* much. I miss her so much.'"

Karen's friend meant well. She was unaware that her own discomfort was behind her suggestion that Karen deny the way she really felt. The friend didn't know that Karen felt isolated and alone when she put on an act.

Here are some suggestions for supporting a friend through a time of grief.

■ *Be there.* If your friend has lost someone to death, go to the funeral if you can. Send a card. Try to be available when your friend wants to talk. It doesn't matter if you have no answers. These small gestures let your friend know that you won't abandon him or her in this time of need.

■ *Let your friend set the pace.* Let him or her decide whether or not to talk and how much. Sometimes your friend may want to share feelings; other times he or she may just want your company.

■ *Acknowledge your friend's pain.* If your friend tells you how much he misses the girlfriend who just dropped him, you might say, "I hear how much you loved her. It must be so hard for you right now." Avoid the temptation to tell him that everything will be OK or that he'll get over it in no time. Right now, everything is *not* OK and "no time" feels like never.

■ *Be aware of your own feelings.* Listening to someone else's pain can bring back memories of times you have felt grieved or sad. This can make you feel uncomfortable or impatient with your friend's pain. If you are aware of these feelings in yourself, you can keep them from influencing how you relate to your friend.

■ *Remember that you can't fix things for your friend — no one can, nor should they.* Grief is healing. It knits together the ragged edges of a torn heart. Over time, your friend will heal, and he or she will thank you for having understood that time was what was needed.

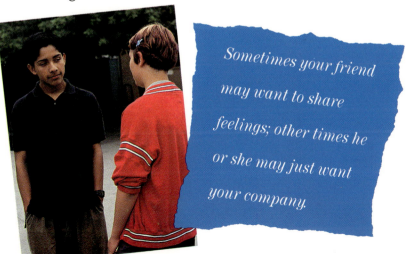

Sometimes your friend may want to share feelings; other times he or she may just want your company.

43

Licensed grief counselors and therapists, as well as some religious leaders, are trained to help people through the grieving process.

A Final Word

This book has described the normal, healthy progress through grief. Unfortunately, not everyone makes this journey successfully. People can run from the pain of grief. They can get stuck at one stage or another along the way.

Someone who still feels nothing many months after a major loss may be stuck in the earliest part of the grieving process. Someone who runs from one activity to another or constantly needs to be with other people may be avoiding dealing with the strong, painful feelings grief brings. Other signs of difficulty with grieving can include drug and alcohol use, truancy, engaging in risky behavior, behaving destructively toward oneself or others, preoccupation with aches and pains, despair or anger that go on without letup for more than six months, and extreme fear of being left alone.

Help is available for people who are having trouble grieving. If you believe you are, reach out. Licensed grief counselors and therapists, as well as some religious leaders, are trained to help people through the grieving process. Getting help is important. Unresolved grief can disrupt your life even years after the loss has occurred. It can rob you of energy and drain the joy from life. It may keep you from forming close relationships or make facing later losses much more difficult. With help, however, you can not only survive your grief but come out stronger for having experienced it.

Over time, the pain of grief gives way to sharing fond, and even funny, memories.

If You'd Like to Learn More

Organizations
The following groups provide information on grieving.

Center for Attitudinal Healing
415-435-5022

Center for Death Education and Research
612-624-1895

Hospice Education Institute
203-767-1620

Books and Movies
Books and movies can help us understand our feelings better.
Here are some that deal with grief and loss.

The Big Wave by Pearl S. Buck (New York: Harper Collins, 1986).
This classic story set in Japan tells how a young boy rebuilds his
life after a tidal wave destroys his village, killing his entire family.

Tiger Eyes by Judy Blume (New York: Dell, 1982). A stranger
helps a young girl face the pain of her father's murder and regain
her interest in life.

Straight Talk About Death for Teenagers by Earl A. Grollman (New
York: Beacon Press, 1993). Written for teens, this book provides
simple explanations of many of the rituals and feelings that
accompany the death of a loved one.

Teens Face to Face with Chronic Illness by Suzanne LeVert (New
York: Julian Messner, 1993). Teenagers talk about how their
illnesses affect their relationships and how they use their own
strength, compassion, and hope to cope with their conditions.

Corrina, Corrina (1994). Whoopi Goldberg stars in this movie
about a nanny who helps a young girl and her father recover from
their grief following the mother's sudden death.

Glossary/Index

aerobic exercise: 39 Activity that requires continuous use of oxygen and benfits the heart and lungs.

dehydrating: 39 Removing water. Drinks that are dehydrating cause the body to eliminate water.

depression: 24 An illness in which a sad mood or loss of pleasure in life, plus other symptoms such as eating and sleeping disorders, lasts without relief for at least two weeks. Depression can lead to suicide and requires professional treatment.

despair: 8 Loss of hope that often occurs when one is grieving over a major loss.

early grief: 14 The period of grieving just after a loss. Shock, denial, and numbness alternating with strong feelings are common during early grief.

empathy: 34 The ability to feel what someone else is feeling.

endorphins: 39 Brain chemicals that are the body's natural painkillers.

general adaptation response: 20 The physical response to any increased demand on the body.

grief: 6 The deep distress caused by a major loss.

grieving process: 14 The stages one typically passes through during grief.

immune system: 38 The body's defense against disease.

listless: 23 Having no energy and no desire to take action of any kind.

major loss: 6 Something of great personal value that is gone from one's life. The death of a loved one, the divorce of one's parents, and damage to one's home due to fire are examples of major losses.

resilient: 16 Able to overcome and grow through adversity.

stress: 38 Any extra demand on the body.

thanatology: 39 The study of death.

toxins: 35 Poisons.